JOURNEY TO THE INNER SELF

THE PHILOSOPHY AND PRACTICE OF INDIAN SPIRITUALITY

DR. JAGADEESH PILLAI

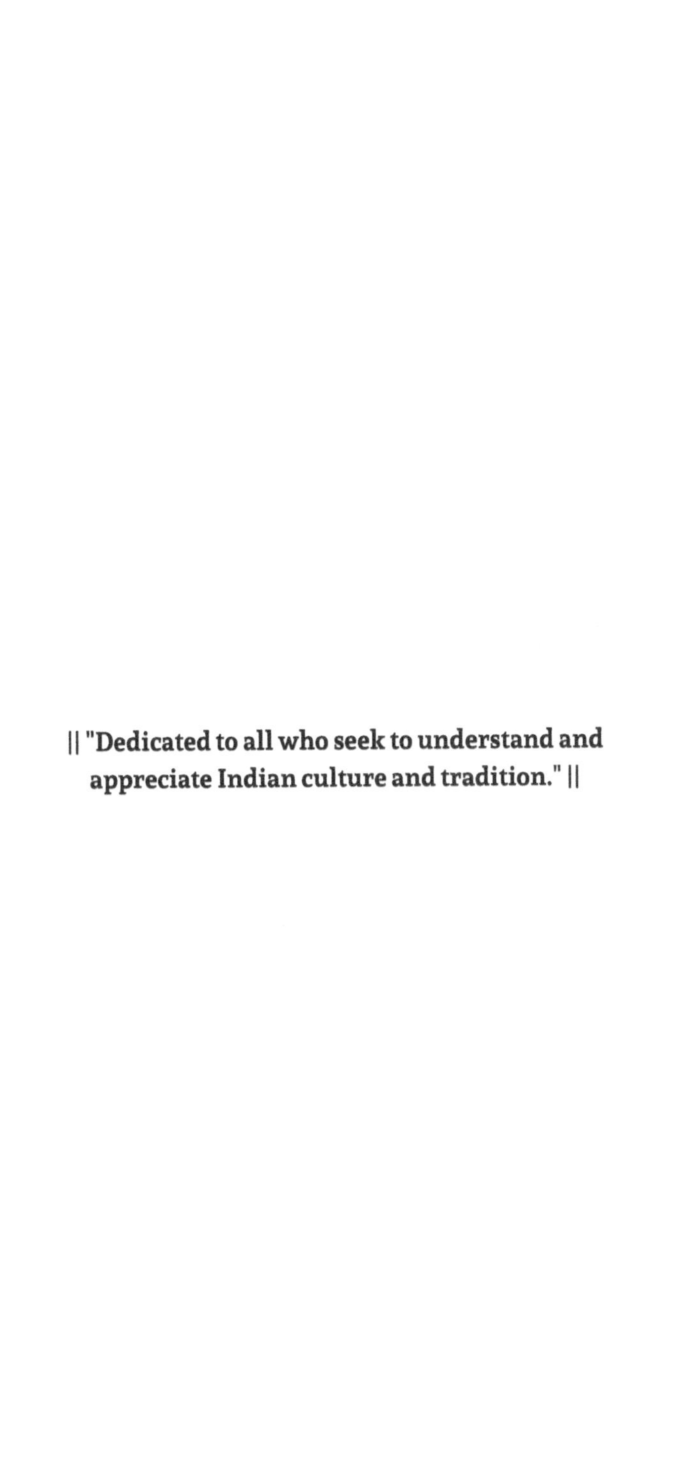

|| "Dedicated to all who seek to understand and appreciate Indian culture and tradition." ||

Contents

Prayer — vii

About The Author — ix

Preface — xiii

1. The Fundamentals Of Indian Spirituality — 1

Part 1

2. The Four Aims Of Life — 7

Part 2

3. The Paths To Liberation — 11

Part 3

4. The Yoga Of Knowledge: A Closer Look At Jnana Yoga — 17

Part 4

5. The Yoga Of Action: A Closer Look At Karma Yoga — 23

Part 5

6. The Yoga Of Devotion: A Closer Look At Bhakti Yoga — 27

Part 6

7. The Yoga Of Self-control: A Closer Look At Raja Yoga — 31

Part 7

8. The Concept Of Maya And The Illusion Of Reality — 37

Part 8

9. The Role Of Meditation In Indian Spirituality — 41

Part 9

Contents

10. Self-realization And Is The Goal Spirituality   47

Part 10

11. The Relevance Of Indian Spirituality In The Modern   51
    World

Other Books Of The Author   55

Contact   59

Prayer

"Om Asato Maa Sadgamaya,Tamaso Maa Jyotir Gamaya,Mrityor Maa Amritam Gamaya, Om Shantih, Shantih, Shantih"

The true meaning of this mantra is: OM guide me from the unreal to the real, from darkness to light, and from mortality to immortality.
OM Peace, Peace, Peace.

ᛩᛩᛩ

About The Author

Dr. Jagadeesh Pillai is a renowned Guinness World Record holder, writer, and researcher hailing from Varanasi, also known as the abode of Lord Shiva. With a Ph.D. in Vedic Science and a range of creative ideas and achievements, he is a true polymath. He is the author of more than 100 books including Research Publications. Although his roots can be traced back to Kerala, the people of Varanasi hold him in high regard and affectionately consider him one of their own.

Dr. Pillai has achieved four Guinness World Records in the following subjects:

"Script to Screen" - In this record, Dr. Pillai produced and directed an animation film within the shortest time possible, breaking the previous record set by Canadians. He has also received numerous national and international awards and recognitions for this achievement.

Longest Line of Postcards - For this record, Dr. Pillai created a line of 16,300 postcards on the occasion of the 163rd anniversary of Indian Postal Day. The event also included a questionnaire about the Indian flag.

Largest Poster Awareness Campaign - Dr. Pillai designed an awareness campaign on the subject of "Beti Bachao - Beti Padhao" (Save the Girl Child - Educate the Girl Child) to achieve this record.

Largest Envelope - In tribute to the Indian Prime Minister's

"Make in India" initiative, Dr. Pillai created a 4000 square meter envelope using waste paper to achieve this record.

Attempted - **70000 Candles on a 210 kg Cake** - To celebrate the 70th Indian Independence Day, Dr. Pillai attempted to light 70,000 candles on a 210 kg cake, which was recorded in World Records India.

Attempted - **Documentary on Dhamek Stupa of Sarnath in 17 Languages** - Dr. Pillai attempted to create a documentary on the Dhamek Stupa of Sarnath, dubbing it in 17 different languages. The result of this attempt is currently awaiting confirmation from the Guinness World Records.

Dr. Pillai is skilled in teaching the Bhagavad Gita, a Hindu scripture, and is popular among young people. He has helped many young people improve their lives through his motivational teachings.

In addition to teaching, he has composed and sung numerous Sanskrit Bhajans and patriotic songs.

He has also written and directed several short films and documentaries for awareness campaigns, and has volunteered with the police in both UP and Kerala to spread awareness about various issues through videos and photography.

Incredibly, he has produced and directed over 100 documentaries about the city of Varanasi, all on his own.

He has also helped and guided more than 25 boys and girls to achieve world records through creative and innovative methods. He is a multifaceted person who uses his intellect and the blessings given to him by God to excel in various areas. He is both a teacher and a student, always learning and teaching, and is able to master any subject he comes across.

He is a selfless social activist and motivational speaker who has overcome struggles and failures to become a successful and enthusiastic individual with a rich life experience.

In addition to his work with the Bhagavad Gita, he is also an efficient Tarot card reader, Astro-Vastu consultant, and a talented singer and composer. He has sung the entire Ram Charita Manas and Bhagavad Gita in his own compositions, and has sung the phrase "Lokah Samastha Sukhino Bhavantu" in 50 different languages. He is currently working on a detailed and scientific study of Vedas, Upanishads, Puranas, and the Bhagavad Gita. He has also composed and sung the Hanuman Chalisa and Gayatri Mantra in 108 and 1008 different compositions, respectively.

Awards - Four Times Guinness World Records, Winner of Mahatma Gandhi Vishwa Shanti Puraskar, Mahatma Gandhi Global Peace Ambassador, Kashi Ratna Award, Dr. APJ Abdul Kalam Motivational Person of the Year 2017, Mother Teresa Award, Indira Gandhi Priyadarshini Award, Bharat Vikas Ratna Award, Udyog Ratna Award, Vigyan Prasar Award, Poorvanchal Ratn Samman.

ॐॐॐ

Preface

"Journey to the Inner Self: The Philosophy and Practice of Indian Spirituality" is a comprehensive guide to understanding and experiencing the ancient wisdom of India. This book delves into the rich and diverse spiritual traditions of India, exploring the philosophical foundations and practical techniques for self-discovery and inner transformation.

The ancient sages and seers of India have left behind a vast treasure trove of knowledge and wisdom that has stood the test of time. They understood the human condition and the nature of the self, and developed powerful practices for attaining inner peace and realization of the ultimate reality.

This book is intended for readers who are interested in exploring the spiritual traditions of India and want to gain a deeper understanding of the philosophy and practices that underlie them. Whether you are a beginner or a seasoned seeker, this book will provide valuable insights and guidance for your own journey to the inner self.

The author has extensively researched the subject and has presented it in an easy to understand language, making it accessible to all. The book covers the major traditions of Indian spirituality such as Yoga, Vedanta, Bhakti and Tantra, and also touches upon lesser known practices like Ayurveda, Jyotish and Vaastu.

This book is not just a theoretical treatise, but also provides practical techniques and exercises that readers can use to experience the benefits of Indian spirituality for themselves. It is a valuable resource for anyone seeking to deepen their understanding of the self and the ultimate reality.

We hope that this book will serve as a guide and companion on your own journey to the inner self. May you find wisdom, peace, and fulfillment in the ancient wisdom of Indian spirituality.

ᐅᐅᐅ

ONE

THE FUNDAMENTALS OF INDIAN SPIRITUALITY

An introduction to the principles and concepts

Indian spirituality is a vast and complex field, with a rich history and a diverse array of practices and traditions. At its core, however, Indian spirituality is rooted in a few fundamental principles and concepts that are common to all of the different traditions. In this chapter, we will explore these fundamentals and gain a better understanding of the underlying philosophy of Indian spirituality.

One of the most fundamental principles of Indian spirituality is the idea of the ultimate reality, or Brahman. Brahman is the absolute and ultimate reality, the ground of all being and the source of all consciousness. It is the unchanging, eternal, and infinite reality that underlies all of existence.

Another key concept in Indian spirituality is the idea of the self, or Atman. According to Indian philosophy, the individual self is not separate from the ultimate reality, but is instead a reflection of it. The goal of Indian spirituality is to realize the unity of the individual self and the ultimate reality, and to attain a state of oneness and non-dual awareness.

The third key concept in Indian spirituality is the idea of karma, or the law of cause and effect. Karma is the principle that every action has a corresponding reaction, and that the actions and choices we make in this life will determine our fate in future lives. The idea of karma is closely tied to the concept of reincarnation, which holds that the individual self is reborn in different forms in a cycle of birth and death.

The fourth key concept in Indian spirituality is the idea of moksha, or liberation. Moksha is the ultimate goal of Indian spirituality, and it refers to the release from the cycle of birth and death and the attainment of a state of spiritual freedom and liberation. According to Indian spirituality, moksha is achieved through the realization of the ultimate reality and the unity of the individual self with it.

Indian spirituality is based on the fundamental principles of the ultimate reality, the self, karma, and moksha. Understanding these concepts is essential for gaining a deeper understanding of the philosophy and practices of

Indian spirituality. In the following chapters, we will explore these concepts in more detail and learn about the different traditions and practices that have developed around them.

ॐॐॐ

"Like the butter hidden in milk, pure consciousness resides within every being, waiting to be revealed through the churning power of the mind. This inner wisdom can be unlocked through contemplation and introspection, allowing us to uncover the hidden depths of our being and discover our true potential." - Amrita-Bindu Upanishad

TWO

THE FOUR AIMS OF LIFE

Understanding the concept of Purushartha"

In Indian spirituality, the concept of Purushartha, or the "four aims of life," is an important principle that guides the individual's spiritual journey. Purushartha is a framework that outlines the four main goals or objectives of human existence: Dharma, Artha, Kama, and Moksha.

The first aim of life, Dharma, refers to the fulfillment of one's moral and ethical responsibilities. It is the principle of living in accordance with one's innate nature and fulfilling one's duty in the world. It is also the foundation of the individual's spiritual practice and the path to inner peace.

The second aim of life, Artha, refers to the pursuit of material wealth and success in the world. It includes the achievement of financial stability, the accumulation of wealth and property, and the attainment of professional success.

The third aim of life, Kama, refers to the satisfaction of one's desires and pleasures. It encompasses the pursuit of pleasure and happiness in the form of love, sex, and other sensual experiences.

The fourth and ultimate aim of life, Moksha, refers to the attainment of spiritual liberation and the realization of the ultimate reality. It is the ultimate goal of Indian spirituality and the ultimate aim of human existence.

The concept of Purushartha is not meant to be a rigid framework but instead, it is a guide to help individuals prioritize their goals and objectives in life. It is important to strive for a balance of the four aims and not to neglect any one of them in favor of the others. It is a reminder that the ultimate goal of human existence is not just material success, but also inner peace and spiritual liberation.

The concept of Purushartha provides a framework for understanding the four main goals or objectives of human existence: Dharma, Artha, Kama, and Moksha, and it serves as a guide to help individuals prioritize their goals and objectives in life.

ဥဥဥ

"You are the embodiment of your deepest, most driving desires. Your will is determined by your desires, and your actions are determined by your will. Ultimately, your destiny is determined by your deeds." - Brihadaranyaka Upanishad

THREE

THE PATHS TO LIBERATION

An overview of different spiritual paths in Indian Spirituality

Indian spirituality is a vast and diverse field, with many different spiritual paths and traditions that have developed over the centuries. Each path has its own unique teachings, practices, and methods for achieving spiritual liberation, also known as Moksha. In this chapter, we will provide an overview of some of the most well-known spiritual paths in Indian spirituality.

The first path is known as the path of knowledge or Jnana Yoga. This path is based on the teachings of the Upanishads and the Vedanta philosophy, which emphasizes the study of sacred texts and the development of self-knowledge and discrimination. The goal of Jnana Yoga is to attain a state of non-dual awareness and to realize the unity of the individual self with the ultimate reality.

The second path is known as the path of devotion or Bhakti Yoga. This path is based on the intense love and devotion to a personal deity or guru. It emphasizes the cultivation of devotion, faith, and surrender as a means to attain spiritual liberation. The goal of Bhakti Yoga is to merge the individual self with the divine through love and devotion.

The third path is known as the path of action or Karma Yoga. This path is based on the principle of selfless service and the performance of one's duties without attachment to the fruits of one's actions. The goal of Karma Yoga is to purify the mind and to attain inner peace and self-control.

The fourth path is known as the path of yoga or Raja Yoga. This path is based on the teachings of Patanjali's Yoga Sutras and emphasizes the practice of physical and mental disciplines, such as meditation and the cultivation of concentration. The goal of Raja Yoga is to attain a state of inner peace and self-control, and to still the fluctuations of the mind.

The fifth path is known as the path of Tantra. It emphasizes the use of rituals, mantras, and visualization as a means to attain spiritual liberation. The goal of Tantra is to merge the individual self with the divine through the use of various spiritual practices and rituals.

Indian spirituality offers many different paths to spiritual liberation, each with its unique teachings, practices, and methods. Some of the most well-known paths include Jnana Yoga, Bhakti Yoga, Karma Yoga, Raja Yoga, and Tantra. Each path has its own unique emphasis, but all ultimately lead to the attainment of spiritual liberation and self-realization.

❦❦❦

To revere our mothers, fathers, teachers, and guests as divine beings is a sacred act. We can honor them by treating them with the utmost respect and admiration, as if they were gods. Doing so is a way of expressing our gratitude for all that they have done for us. It is also a way of showing our appreciation for the wisdom and guidance they have provided us. By treating them with reverence, we can demonstrate our commitment to upholding the highest standards of morality and integrity. - The Taittiriya Upanishad

FOUR

THE YOGA OF KNOWLEDGE: A CLOSER LOOK AT JNANA YOGA

Jnana Yoga, also known as the "yoga of knowledge," is one of the most ancient and respected spiritual paths in Indian spirituality. It is based on the teachings of the Upanishads and the Vedanta philosophy, which emphasizes the development of self-knowledge and discrimination as a means to attain spiritual liberation.

Jnana Yoga is a path that is based on the pursuit of knowledge and wisdom. It is a path of self-inquiry, in which the seeker seeks to understand the nature of the self and the ultimate reality. This is done through the study of sacred texts, such as the Upanishads and the Bhagavad Gita, as well as through the practice of meditation and self-reflection.

The goal of Jnana Yoga is to attain a state of non-dual awareness, in which the individual realizes the unity of the self with the ultimate reality. This realization is known as "Brahman-jnana," or the knowledge of Brahman. In this state, the individual experiences a deep sense of inner peace, joy, and fulfillment, and is released from the cycle of birth and death.

One of the key teachings of Jnana Yoga is the idea of "neti, neti," which means "not this, not this." This teaching is based on the idea that the ultimate reality cannot be described or defined, and that it is not the same as the physical or mental world. The seeker must negate or reject all concepts and ideas about the self and the ultimate reality in order to arrive at the true understanding of them.

Jnana Yoga is considered to be one of the most difficult and rigorous spiritual paths. It requires a deep commitment to the pursuit of knowledge, a strong will, and a good deal of self-discipline. It is a path that is best suited for those who have a deep interest in philosophy and a strong desire to understand the ultimate reality.

Jnana Yoga is one of the most ancient and respected spiritual paths in Indian spirituality, which is based on the pursuit of knowledge and wisdom, through the study of sacred texts, meditation, and self-inquiry. The goal of Jnana Yoga is to attain a state of non-dual awareness and to realize the unity of the individual self with the ultimate reality. It is considered a challenging path but for those who are inclined towards philosophy and have a strong desire to understand the ultimate reality, it is a path that is worth pursuing.

❥❥❥

The body is said to be a temple, and the soul is truly Shiva. Discard the faded flower offerings of ignorance and instead worship with the thought: "I am He". – Maitreya Upanishad

FIVE

THE YOGA OF ACTION: A CLOSER LOOK AT KARMA YOGA

Karma Yoga, also known as the "yoga of action," is a spiritual path in Indian spirituality that emphasizes the importance of performing one's actions in a selfless and detached manner. It is based on the principle of selfless service and the performance of one's duties without attachment to the fruits of one's actions. The Karma Yoga is closely connected with the 3rd chapter of Bhagavad Gita, which is also known as "Karma Yoga."

The goal of Karma Yoga is to purify the mind and to attain inner peace and self-control. It is based on the belief that actions performed with a pure and selfless motivation have the power to bring about spiritual transformation. By performing actions in this way, the individual can detach themselves from the ego and the desire for personal gain, and instead, act in accordance with the will of the divine.

Karma Yoga is not just about performing good deeds, but also about the mindset and attitude with which the actions are performed. The Karma Yoga encourages the individual to approach all actions with a sense of detachment and non-attachment, and to perform them without any expectation of reward or recognition. The goal is to perform actions for the sake of the action itself and not for personal gain.

The Bhagavad Gita, one of the most important texts of Hinduism, is a dialogue between Lord Krishna and Arjuna, in which Lord Krishna explains the concept of Karma Yoga. The third chapter of Bhagavad Gita, which is known as "Karma Yoga" specifically deals with this path, Lord Krishna explains to Arjuna the importance of performing one's actions with a sense of duty and detachment, and how this can lead to spiritual liberation.

Karma Yoga is a spiritual path that emphasizes the importance of performing one's actions in a selfless and detached manner. The goal is to purify the mind and to attain inner peace and self-control. It is closely connected with the 3rd chapter of Bhagavad Gita, which specifically deals with this path. By performing actions with a sense of duty and detachment, the individual can detach themselves from the ego and the desire for personal gain and act in accordance with the will of the divine.

ᵱᵱᵱ

Those who recognize the unity of all life, seeing themselves in all creatures and all creatures in themselves, know no fear or grief. How can the multiplicity of life deceive the one who perceives its oneness? – Isha Upanishad

SIX

THE YOGA OF DEVOTION: A CLOSER LOOK AT BHAKTI YOGA

Bhakti Yoga, also known as the "yoga of devotion," is a spiritual path in Indian spirituality that emphasizes the cultivation of devotion, faith, and surrender as a means to attain spiritual liberation. It is based on the intense love and devotion to a personal deity or guru. Bhakti Yoga is closely connected with the 12th chapter of Bhagavad Gita, which is also known as "Yoga of Devotion"

The goal of Bhakti Yoga is to merge the individual self with the divine through love and devotion. It is based on the belief that the divine is present within all things and that devotion is the path to realizing this truth. The Bhakti Yoga encourages the individual to approach all actions with a sense of devotion and to cultivate a deep and personal relationship with the divine.

The Bhagavad Gita, one of the most important texts of Hinduism, is a dialogue between Lord Krishna and Arjuna, in which Lord Krishna explains the concept of Bhakti Yoga. The 12th chapter of Bhagavad Gita, which is known as "Yoga of Devotion" specifically deals with this path, Lord Krishna explains to Arjuna the importance of devotion and how it can lead to spiritual liberation.

Bhakti Yoga is a path that is open to all individuals, regardless of their background or caste. It is a path that is accessible to people from all walks of life and can be practiced by anyone who has a sincere desire to connect with the divine. It is considered a path of the heart and is said to be the easiest path to spiritual liberation.

Bhakti Yoga is a spiritual path that emphasizes the cultivation of devotion, faith, and surrender as a means to attain spiritual liberation. It is closely connected with the 12th chapter of Bhagavad Gita, which specifically deals with this path. The goal of Bhakti Yoga is to merge the individual self with the divine through love and devotion. It is considered a path of the heart, accessible to people from all walks of life and is said to be the easiest path to spiritual liberation.

ϷϷϷ

The consequences of one's actions determine their character. Through virtuous actions, one becomes virtuous, and through bad actions, one becomes bad. – Brihadaranyaka Upanishad

SEVEN

The Yoga of Self-Control: A closer look at Raja Yoga

Raja Yoga, also known as the "yoga of self-control," is a spiritual path in Indian spirituality that emphasizes the practice of physical and mental disciplines, such as meditation and the cultivation of concentration. It is based on the teachings of Patanjali's Yoga Sutras and is considered one of the most systematic and complete paths to spiritual liberation. Raja Yoga is closely connected with the 11th chapter of Bhagavad Gita, which is also known as "Raja Vidya Raja Guhya Yogam", the king of secrets hidden with us.

The goal of Raja Yoga is to attain a state of inner peace and self-control, and to still the fluctuations of the mind. It is based on the belief that the mind is the root cause of all suffering and that by stilling the mind, the individual can achieve inner peace and spiritual liberation. The Raja Yoga involves the practice of various techniques such as asanas, pranayama, and dhyana (meditation) to control the mind and body.

The Bhagavad Gita, one of the most important texts of Hinduism, is a dialogue between Lord Krishna and Arjuna, in which Lord Krishna explains the concept of Raja Yoga. The 11th chapter of Bhagavad Gita, which is known as "Raja Vidya Raja Guhya Yogam" specifically deals with this path, Lord Krishna explains to Arjuna the importance of self-control and how it can lead to spiritual liberation.

Raja Yoga is considered to be one of the most challenging paths as it requires a great deal of self-discipline and commitment. It is a path that is best suited for individuals who are looking for a systematic and structured approach to spiritual practice. The Raja Yoga is a path that leads to the control of the mind and ultimately the attainment of self-realization.

Raja Yoga, also known as the "yoga of self-control," is a spiritual path that emphasizes the practice of physical and mental disciplines, such as meditation and the cultivation of concentration. It is closely connected with the 11th chapter of Bhagavad Gita, which specifically deals with this path. The goal of Raja Yoga is to attain a state of inner peace and self-control, and to still the fluctuations of the mind. It is considered one of the most challenging paths, but for those who are committed and disciplined, it leads to the ultimate goal of self-realization.

ᗡᗡᗡ

Just as the sun, the eye of the world, is not tainted by the defects of our eyes or the objects it looks upon, the one Self, dwelling in all, is not tainted by the evils of the world, for it transcends all. – Katha Upanishad

EIGHT

THE CONCEPT OF MAYA AND THE ILLUSION OF REALITY

The concept of Maya is an important principle in Indian spirituality and philosophy. It refers to the idea that the world we perceive and experience is not the ultimate reality, but rather an illusion or a projection of the mind. Maya is often described as a veil or a curtain that covers the true reality, and it is through the attainment of spiritual knowledge that the individual can see beyond this veil and realize the ultimate reality.

The illusion of reality is the idea that what we perceive as the external world is not real, but rather a projection of the mind. The idea is that the mind creates an illusory reality based on its own limitations, and that the individual is trapped in this illusion, unable to see the true reality.

The concept of Maya is closely connected with the idea of duality, which states that the individual self and the ultimate reality are separate and distinct. The illusion of reality is the result of the individual's identification with the ego, which creates a sense of separation between the self and the ultimate reality.

The ultimate goal of Indian spirituality is to transcend the illusion of reality and to realize the ultimate reality, which is beyond the mind and the ego. This is done through the cultivation of spiritual knowledge, the attainment of self-knowledge and discrimination, and the practice of spiritual disciplines such as meditation and self-inquiry.

The concept of Maya refers to the idea that the world we perceive and experience is an illusion or a projection of the mind. The illusion of reality is the idea that what we perceive as the external world is not real, but rather a projection of the mind. The ultimate goal of Indian spirituality is to transcend the illusion of reality and to realize the ultimate reality, which is beyond the mind and the ego. This is done through the cultivation of spiritual knowledge, the attainment of self-knowledge and discrimination, and the practice of spiritual disciplines such as meditation and self-inquiry.

ᐅᐅᐅ

As the same fire takes on different shapes when it consumes objects of varying shapes, so does the one Self take the shape of every creature in whom it is present. – Katha Upanishad

NINE

THE ROLE OF MEDITATION IN INDIAN SPIRITUALITY

Techniques and practices

Meditation is an integral part of Indian spirituality, and is considered to be one of the most powerful tools for spiritual development and self-realization. Meditation is a practice that involves the cultivation of concentration and mindfulness, and it is through the practice of meditation that the individual can gain insight into the nature of the self and the ultimate reality.

There are several different types of meditation techniques and practices in Indian spirituality, each with its own unique emphasis and approach. Some of the most well-known practices include:

Transcendental Meditation: This is a simple and effortless technique that involves the repetition of a mantra or sound, which allows the mind to enter a state of deep relaxation and inner stillness.

Jnana Yoga: This is a path of self-inquiry that emphasizes the study of sacred texts and the development of self-knowledge and discrimination.

Raja Yoga: This is a path that emphasizes the practice of physical and mental disciplines, such as meditation and the cultivation of concentration.

Bhakti Yoga: This is a path of devotion that emphasizes the cultivation of devotion, faith, and surrender.

Vipassana Meditation: This is a form of insight meditation that emphasizes the cultivation of mindfulness and the observation of one's thoughts, emotions, and physical sensations.

Each of these techniques and practices has its own unique emphasis, but all of them are designed to help the individual to still the mind, to achieve a state of inner peace and self-control, and to gain insight into the nature of the self and the ultimate reality.

One of the most important things to keep in mind when practicing meditation is to maintain a consistent and regular practice. The benefits of meditation are cumulative, and it is important to set aside time each day to practice. It is also important to find a quiet and comfortable place to meditate, where you can be free from distractions.

Another important aspect of meditation is to maintain an open and receptive attitude, and to approach the practice with a sense of curiosity and non-judgment. It is also important to be patient and not to expect immediate results. Meditation is a process, and it takes time and practice to see the benefits.

Meditation is an integral part of Indian spirituality, and is considered to be one of the most powerful tools for spiritual development and self-realization. There are several different types of meditation techniques and practices in Indian spirituality, each with its own unique emphasis and approach. To practice meditation, it's important to have consistency and discipline, maintain an open and receptive attitude, and to be patient and not to expect immediate results. It's a process that requires time and practice to see the benefits.

ррр

Like a spider spinning forth its thread and drawing it back in, the entire creation is woven from Brahman and unto it returns. – Mundaka Upanishad

TEN

SELF-REALIZATION AND IS THE GOAL SPIRITUALITY

Self-realization is the ultimate goal of Indian spirituality, and it refers to the process of realizing one's true nature and the ultimate reality. Indian spirituality teaches that the individual self is not separate from the ultimate reality, but is in fact one and the same. The ultimate goal of Indian spirituality is to help the individual to realize this truth and to merge the individual self with the ultimate reality.

Self-realization is achieved through the cultivation of spiritual knowledge, the attainment of self-knowledge and discrimination, and the practice of spiritual disciplines such as meditation and self-inquiry. It is through these practices that the individual can see beyond the illusion of reality and realize the true nature of the self and the ultimate reality.

In Indian spirituality, self-realization is often described as a state of non-dual awareness, in which the individual realizes the unity of the self with the ultimate reality. This realization is known as "Brahman-jnana," or the knowledge of Brahman. In this state, the individual experiences a deep sense of inner peace, joy, and fulfillment, and is released from the cycle of birth and death.

Self-realization is considered to be the ultimate goal of Indian spirituality because it is the realization of one's true nature and the ultimate reality. It is the ultimate goal because it leads to the attainment of inner peace, self-control, and the release from the cycle of birth and death.

Self-realization is the ultimate goal of Indian spirituality and refers to the process of realizing one's true nature and the ultimate reality. Indian spirituality teaches that the individual self is not separate from the ultimate reality, but is in fact one and the same. Self-realization is achieved through the cultivation of spiritual knowledge, the attainment of self-knowledge and discrimination, and the practice of spiritual disciplines such as meditation and self-inquiry. It is considered the ultimate goal of Indian spirituality because it leads to the attainment of inner peace, self-control, and release from the cycle of birth and death.

ᢣᢣᢣ

The wise man beholds all beings in the self and the self in all beings; for that reason, they do not hate anyone. – Isha Upanishad

ELEVEN

THE RELEVANCE OF INDIAN SPIRITUALITY IN THE MODERN WORLD

An analysis of how traditional spiritual practices can be integrated in modern life.

Indian spirituality, with its emphasis on self-realization and the cultivation of inner peace, has a relevance and a significance that is timeless. However, in a fast-paced, modern world, it can be a challenge to integrate traditional spiritual practices into our daily lives.

One way that traditional spiritual practices can be integrated into modern life is by making them a part of our daily routine. For example, starting the day with a few minutes of meditation or pranayama (breathing exercises) can help to set the tone for the day and to bring a sense of inner peace and balance.

Another way to integrate traditional spiritual practices into modern life is by incorporating them into our work and daily activities. For example, one can approach their work with a sense of detachment and non-attachment, as taught in Karma Yoga, or to approach it with a sense of devotion, as taught in Bhakti Yoga.

Additionally, many spiritual practices such as yoga, meditation, and pranayama can be adapted to be practiced in modern settings, like yoga classes, meditation apps, and online tutorials.

Indian spirituality also emphasizes the importance of living in harmony with nature, and this is a principle that is especially relevant in today's world. By living in harmony with nature, we can reduce our impact on the environment and create a more sustainable world for future generations.

Indian spirituality, with its emphasis on self-realization and the cultivation of inner peace, has a relevance and significance that is timeless. However, in a fast-paced, modern world, it can be challenging to integrate traditional spiritual practices into our daily lives. One way to do this is by making them a part of our daily routine, incorporating them into our work and daily activities and adapting them to be practiced in modern settings. Additionally, living in harmony with nature is an important principle of Indian spirituality, which is especially relevant in today's world.

❧❧❧

Other Books Of The Author

1. The Moments When I Met God
2. Kashiyile Theertha Pathangal
3. GURU GYAN VANI
4. Abhiprerak Gita
5. ASSI SE JAIN GHAT TAK
6. Hopelessness of Arjuna
7. The Soul and It's True Nature
8. Sense of Action (Karma)
9. Action through Wisdom
10. Action through Wisdom
11. THEORY AND PRACTICAL OF EVERY ACTION
12. LOGICAL UNDERSTANDING OF THE SUPREME
13. THE IMPERISHABLE SUPREME
14. Yatra Nishadraj se Hanuman Ghat Tak
15. Yatra Karnatak Ghat se Raja Ghat Tak
16. Yatra Pandey Ghat se Prayagraj Ghat Tak
17. Yatra Ranjendra Prasad Ghat se Dattatreya Ghat Tak
18. YaatraSindhiya Ghat se Gwaliar Ghat Tak
19. Yatra Mangala Gauri Ghat se Hanuman Gadhi Ghat Tak
20. Yatra Gaay Ghat Se Nishad Ghat Tak
21. MAA GANGA, GHATEN EVM UTSAV
22. Ganga Arti Dev Deepavali evam Any Utsav
23. Potentials of Digitalized India
24. VEDIC CONSCIOUSNESS
25. A Brief Introduction to Vedic Science
26. Kashi ke Barah Jyotirling
27. IMPACT OF MOTIVATION
28. Let's have a Milky Way Journey
29. Color Therapy in a Nutshell

30. Rigveda in a Nutshell
31. Yajurveda in a Nutshell
32. Samveda in a Nutshell
33. Atharva Veda in a Nutshell
34. Ayushman Bhava - Ayurveda
35. Srimad Bhagavad Gita and Upanishad Connection
36. Srimad Bhagavad Gita - an attempt to summarize each chapter.
37. Facts and Impact of Nakshatra
38. Astro Gems - NAVARATNA
39. Ekadashi - A Concise Overview
40. A Concise View of Hanuman Chalisa
41. Inspirational Gita
42. Nakshatraranyam
43. Summary of 18 Mahapuranas
44. Synopsis of 18 Upa Puranas
45. Rigvediya Upanishads
46. Shukla Yajurvediya Upanishads
47. Krishna Yajurvediya Upanishads
48. Samavediya Upanishads
49. Atharvavediya Upanishads
50. The Seven Great Sages
51. From Rocket Scientist to President Dr. APJ Abdul Kalam
52. The Visionary's Voice - Quotes of Dr. APJ Abdul Kalam
53. The Wisdom of Swami Vivekananda: Insights and Inspiration from a Legendary Spiritual Teacher
54. Ayurvedic Remedies from the Garden
55. Sages and Seers
56. Rising Strong – Motivational Stories of Women
57. Beyond Flames -Mystery stories of Funeral Ghat Manikarnika
58. The Origins of Tulsi: A Look at the Mythological Roots of the Plant"

59. The Holistic Cow: A Look at the Physical, Spiritual, and Cultural Importance of Cows in India
60. Arts of Healing
61. Exploring the Divine
62. Understanding Five Elements
63. The Etymology of Ram
64. Symbols of India
65. Voice of Change (About Speeches of Great Men)
66. She Speaks (About Speeches of Great Women)
67. **Patriotism on Celluloid – Brief About Patriotic Films**
68. **The Music of Motivation: A Brief Guide to Inspirational Film Songs**
69. **Unlocking the Secrets of the Dashopanishads**
70. A Cultural Mosaic
71. **Ancient Traditions, Modern Minds**
72. **Beneath the Surface**
73. **From Temples to Ashrams**

❧❧❧

Contact

DR. JAGADEESH PILLAI

PhD in Vedic Science

Four Times Guinness World Record Holder

Winner of Mahatma Gandhi Vishwa Shanti Puraskar and
Global Peace Ambassador

Gemology, Astro & Vastu Consultant - Spiritual Counselor

Consultant for designing World Record Ideas

Efficient Tarot Card Reader

9839093003

myrichindia@gmail.com

drjagadeeshpillai@facebook

drjagadeeshpillai@instagram

jagadeeshpillai@youtube

www. JAGADEESHPILLAI.com

ꙮꙮꙮ

|| LOKAHA SAMASTHAHA SUKHINO BHAVANTU ||

• 61 •